A Napa ChristChild

—AND—

BENICIA'S LETTERS

CHARLES A. GUNNISON

[ZHINGOORA BOOKS]

This edition is published by
Zhingoora Books.

The Cover is Designed by Pallav Sethiya.

CONTENTS

- A NAPA CHRISTCHILD.

    o I.

    o II.

    o III.

    o IV.

- BENICIA'S LETTERS.

A Napa Christchild.

I.

An evening sky, broken by wandering clouds, which hastening onward toward the north, bear their rich gifts of longed-for rain to the brown meadows, filling the heavens from east to west with graceful lines and swelling bosoms, save, just at the horizon where the sun descended paints a broad, lurid streak of crimson, glowing amid the deepening shadows, a coal in dead, gray ashes.

Darker grows the streak, as a stain of blood, while the clouds about it now assume a purple tinge with gloomier shadings; suddenly in the centre of the lurid field starts out as if that moment born to Earth, with clear, silver light, the Evening Star. The colour slowly fades till all is dead and ashy, and the silver star drops down below the purpled hills, leaving for a moment a soft, trembling twilight; the dense clouds then rolling in between, blot out the last sign of departed day and night is come.

It was Christmas Eve. The winter was late, and rain had fallen during the last few weeks only, so that the fields were just assuming the fresh pea-green colour of their new life, and the long, dead grass still standing above the recent growth gave that odd smokey appearance to the hills and mesas, so familiar to all us Californians also in our olive groves. The night, however, was dark and nothing of hills, or mesas, or gray fields, could be seen as the hurrying bands of clouds joined together in one great company, overspreading the whole sky and clothing all in a dreary shroud of blackness.

The little arroyo, which was dry in the summertime, had now risen, increased by last week's tribute to be quite a large stream, tearing noisily among the rocks and over its old courses, giving friendly greetings of recognition to the old water-marks and dashing a playful wave now and then about the worn roots of the enormous laurel tree whose branches reached high above and far around.

Beneath the tree's protecting limbs, a little cabin, of roughest workmanship, found shelter from the wind, or shade from the intense heat of summer; the house was built almost entirely of logs, excepting the upper part where boards had been used and through which were cut the three windows which served to light the single room it contained.

This Christmas Eve, only the dark form of the cabin was to be seen with the tall adobe chimney built up the outside; the smoke blew, beaten here and there, about the roof till it finally disappeared, a cloud of ghosts, among the swaying branches of the laurel tree.

By day in the sunshine, no pleasanter spot could be found than the little cabin and broad fields of Crescimir the Illyrian, no lovelier view of the rich Napa Valley could be had than from the hill where Crescimir's cattle grazed and no happier home could have been found in all the Californias than his, had he not been so alone, without a friend and far from his native country.

On the very day which opens this story, one might have stood upon the bridge and watched the lazy flowing of the river on whose dull green surface all the spans and bars were shadowed, and on the buttress seen the sunshine in ever changing, trembling glints of gold. Dead thistles were on the bank rustling in the breeze and the long tules by the water-side, some broken, others upright, waved gracefully, moved by both wind and current. To the left hand on both sides of the arroyo which here joined the river, one could have seen Crescimir's fields and the vegetable garden with its whitey-green cabbages, the rich brown heaps of manure and straw, and the beds of beets all crimson and green, then the borders of oaks and the far, blue hills, while myriads of little gray-winged moths hovered over the masses of tangled blackberry vines and giant dock. To the southward rose, far away, the peak of glorious Tamalpais, a dark blue dash without a shadow. There were the black, ploughed fields, steaming in the sunshine, larks springing up from the glittering leaves, and noisy squirrels in the bay tree laying away their stores of nuts and maize in its hundred hollows. Leaning upon the rail and watching the river, rippled in the centre but calm and glassy near the banks, one could have seen the silver fish springing from the water for the insects playing about the surface, and could have breathed the rich perfume of growing onions and the sweet, fresh, green life.

On the hillside Crescimir had planted grape vines, but they were young yet and bore no fruit, still, had they borne the heaviest of clusters there was no one to eat them then for there were but few settlers in the valley and Crescimir had no neighbours, but the Rancho Tulucay, nearer than the little village three miles distant.

Thus Crescimir the Illyrian lived alone improving his lands and selling vegetables to the Yankee traders who came up the river in their little schooners; he was always busy ploughing and dressing the gardens or clearing away the chaparral.

Two years had been spent here since he had left his fatherland, amid the wild scenes of the Julian Alps. It was on a Christmas Eve that he had bidden his old friends good bye and at each return of the day he thought more sadly of his lonely life, sighing for the old mountain village where he had so often made merry with his comrades.

There was one bright spot in Crescimir's daily routine and he prized that above all the day, for it showed to him that there was one person who did think of him, though who he could never learn. For a year or more he had found each day at his cabin door a bunch of garden flowers and in their place he daily left a bunch of his sweetest onions or some rare vegetable, which were always taken away.

The rain began to fall, after Crescimir, having made the horse and cattle right for the night, started to his cabin. The barn was on the summit of the knoll, at the foot of which, by the arroyo, he had built his little house of one room.

Crescimir felt his way along through the vegetable garden, carrying the milk pail in one hand and holding the lantern out before him with the other; the light glistened upon the tall stalks of last year's maize and gleamed back from the glossy, pungent leaves of the bay tree, from the tin pail and his wet boots, all reflected in the little pools fast collecting in the path. As he neared the cabin the rain fell as it seldom does, save in the tropics, and Crescimir entering the cabin closed the door with a noise, warning the storm not to encroach on the little bit of the world which was his own.

Inside the cabin there was a blazing wood-fire on the open hearth and a lighted candle on the table; the interior was homelike and comfortable; in one corner stood the bed with white cover, there were two arm chairs, a tall dresser and two tables, one of the tables set for supper, which consisted simply of bread and milk which Crescimir was ready for as soon as he had washed his hands at the pump in the little "lean-to," and exchanged his long boots for a pair of easy slippers.

Over the fireplace hung a bunch of crimson toyone berries and a branch of hemlock, which Crescimir had hung there to mark the holiday. He did not sit down at once to his meal, but stood, leaning against the chimney piece, meditatively picking off bits of the hemlock and throwing them into the fire where they crackled with a merry noise and blazed up, scenting the room with their fragrance of the forest.

As he threw the bits into the fire he sang that melody which the Illyrian children sing when bearing home their Christmas trees, found always in the deep forests; it was a song dear to him and the words brought up memories of all his happy home life and he grew sad as he thought of the lonely present.

"Deep in the wilds of Illyria's mountains

Under a hemlock tree,

Good Spirits buried a wonderful treasure,

Long years ago for me.

There in the gloom by a snow-born fountain

We found the hemlock tree,

Bore it away with loud notes of pleasure,

Hearts overrunning with glee.

Here is my hemlock tree

Christchild kiss it for me,

Make every branch bear

A gift that is fair,

This glossy-leaved hemlock tree,

Evergreen hemlock tree.

Hemlock ne'er blooms unless kissed by the Christchild,

Glossy-leaved hemlock tree!

Come little Christchild and breathe on its branches

That its fair blossoms we see;

Kissed by the lips of the Heavenly Christchild,

Blessed by the wind so free,

Grown o'er the treasure the Good Spirits planted

Wondrous its fruit must be!

Here is my hemlock tree,

Christchild kiss it for me.

Make every branch bear

A gift that is fair,

This glossy-leaved hemlock tree,

Evergreen hemlock tree."

"Alas for me," exclaimed Crescimir, "my happy Christchild days are over and I fear he has forgotten where I live out in Alta California and will never bring me anything again."

Just as the song was finished, a sound was heard at the door but Crescimir thinking that it was the wind, gave no attention to it, sitting down to his supper.

He had not eaten the first spoonful of his bread and milk when the door opened and by the aid of the firelight, for the draught extinguished the candle, he saw a pretty, little, golden haired child in a short, white frock which reached to the knees; the child wore neither hat, shoes, nor stockings and, what seemed most remarkable, was dry despite the heavy rain. The little creature as quietly closed the door as he had opened it, and smiling, walked up to the hearth, spreading out before it his tiny, pink hands.

II.

As the little visitor stretched out his hands to warm them at the fire, his shadow formed a flickering cross upon the floor. Crescimir noticed this, and also wondering at the mysterious advent of the child, which coming so closely upon his song, caused him almost to think that he must be dreaming.

"Art thou the Christchild?" he said finally, to the little figure which stood with its back toward him gazing up at the branch of hemlock above the fireplace.

The child turned around and looking merrily at Crescimir, broke into a fit of boisterous laughter, but did not answer.

"Thou art not a very polite little boy, to break into a house this way and then not answer a simple question. Thou art no Austrian

Christchild, I am sure of that. No matter," he added, as he saw the little face pucker up for a cry, "wait till we are better acquainted and then we can talk it all over."

The child smiled again and made a sign indicating that he wanted the hemlock branch above his head. Crescimir took it down for him and as soon as the little creature received it, he began hopping about the room, holding the branch aloft and humming the melody which Crescimir had just been singing.

"Truly, thou art a strange little elf, but I know how to tell if thou art mortal. Wilt thou have thy supper?" and he held out a spoonful of the bread and milk to the dancing figure. The child immediately stopped his whirling, and running to Crescimir, eagerly ate the food, and then climbing into his lap, sat there quietly, with expectant face as if anticipating a share in the rest of the supper. So Crescimir took one spoonful and the Christchild the next, until the bowl was empty.

"I am glad that thou art come, little one," said Crescimir, as he held the child in his arms, seated in the wooden armchulr before the fire. "Thou hast made my Christmas Eve a very pleasant one, but I wish that I could know who thou art and whether thy parents are anxiously searching for thee this stormy night. Canst thou not speak?"

The child shook his golden head solemnly and began throwing bits of the hemlock into the flames, watching the blaze they made as if he could read in it.

Crescimir had spoken in German and the little waif understood him, but it seemed that he was unable to answer except in a cooing sound expressive of his sensations; however, he could sing most sweetly, not articulating, but singing as a bird and making beautiful melody. The song which Crescimir had been singing when he entered, seemed to please his ear greatly and he warbled it over again in his strangely sweet tones. Crescimir sung the song a number of times to him and also many others, some of which with their merry music, breathing fresh from the high Alps, caused his little hand to keep time with the hemlock branch as he joined in the songs with his curious notes.

"Thou art a little elf!" exclaimed Crescimir as he kissed the rosy face. "Thou bringest back all the old days and makest me feel as merry as I used in far off Illyria. Bless thee little Christchild."

The mysterious guest laughed gaily pulling Crescimir's hair and drawing his smooth fingers over the dark, weather beaten face of the man. Then he played horse, riding on Crescimir's knee using the branch for a whip, while Crescimir sang little verses which came to his mind, verses which set to rolicking music he had sung in his old home on feast days at dances in the tavern, accompanied by zither or hackbretl.

"My girl has ta'en her love away,

I'm easier now I guess,

Don't have to go so oft to church,

Nor half so oft confess—

Nor half so oft confess."

The wind blew harder but neither Crescimir nor his guest heeded it, while the roaring of the arroyo and river and the steady pouring of the rain on the roof did not mar their merry making in the least, and they laughed and sung regardless of it all.

"Now I have two girls,

An old one and a new,

So now I need two hearts,

A false one and a true."

He continued:

"Here Heavenly Father,

'T were fine to remain

If for just half an hour

'T would gold dollars rain."

Just then the little cabin shook.

"Strong wind to-night; it is lucky for thee, Christchild, that thou hast found shelter and lucky for me that the evening which promised to be so dull has been a very merry one.

"Don't be so sad, boy,

If she did treat thee rough,

The world is like a hen-roost,

Has pullets quite enough."

Crescimir ceased singing, for the Christchild stopped suddenly in his romping, gazing fixedly with his large, wondering eyes upon the floor.

"What see'st thou, little one?"

The child pointed to the door and Crescimir saw two small streams of white, foamy water pouring in from each side, and the floor was covered. Crescimir quickly placed the Christchild on the table and started to open the door, but before he reached it, the house trembled as if in an earthquake shock and the door fell back into the room with a loud crash, while a volume of seething water washed over it almost throwing him down with its terrible force. The water poured in little jets through the cracks in the walls and rushing into the fireplace put out the flames and left the room in total darkness.

The water rose rapidly and by the time that Crescimir had grasped the form of his little guest and opening one of the windows had drawn himself with his charge upon the roof, the flood had reached the upper sashes.

The cabin swayed to and fro and every moment seemed about to be carried from its foundations. The Christchild made no sound of fear and Crescimir could not see his face, yet he held the long hemlock branch tightly in his little hand.

The roof was firmly built of logs and planks so in case the house fell it could be used as a raft and Crescimir exerting all his strength pulled from the sides the flat boards which held it fixed to the cabin.

As the flood rose higher, he took the Christchild and lying down in the middle of the roof held on firmly.

Suddenly the roof was lifted and whirled down the swollen arroyo into the broad river. Floating logs struck against it, and as they tore along under the bridge they struck against the buttress with terrific force. Onward they were whirled; they could see the lights in the houses of the village and could hear the voices of men and women along the bluffs or in the trees where they had sought shelter.

The rain ceased falling, but the wind did not go down, rolling the waves over their raft. Once they lodged for a moment against a great oak where Crescimir strove in vain to make fast. The tide was too powerful and all went with it whirling blindly onward.

III.

The waters fell almost as rapidly as they had risen, and by sunrise on Christmas Day, the river had returned between its banks, though still flowing fast and frothy.

Mists lay in strata along the hills showing the green grass between in long, even stripes. Up from the high mesas sprang the larks ready to greet the day, or perching for a moment on some sturdy manzanita they spread their broad tails, with two white feathers, balancing and chirping cheerily. A little valley through which an arroyo flowed, scantily bordered by low growing willows, formed the scene; on one side was a stubble-field with many cattle grazing on the new grass; there were a few dark oaks and then on the first risings, yellow patches of vineyards with red, ploughed ground dotted with manzanitas. The high hills which formed the background were rough and black.

In the hollow at the foot of the mesa was a newly formed pond on which floated branches of trees, bits of wood and some broken pieces of household furniture; about the grass was strewn the same sort of drift and the grass itself was torn and bent and there were yellow-white bits of foam upon it. At one side wedged between two encina trees lay the roof of a house, on the edge of which a little child was sitting beside the body of a man, who lying with one arm hunglistlessly over the side seemed asleep or dead. The pond was fast lowering, leaving its burden of debris scattered about.

This was the scene which met the searching eyes of Jovita of Tulucay Rancho as, mounted on her horse, she came around the knoll which hid the house and buildings of the rancho from the meadow.

Jovita quickly alighted, took up the child in her arms, and seeing that he was unhurt but simply dazed at his situation, placed him upon her horse and gave her attention to the man who lay there, to all appearances dead.

"Unfortunate man," she said aloud, unable to repress her tears, "his wife has probably been lost and he has saved their child."

She took his hand in hers and felt that his pulse was yet beating; a bruise on the temple seemed to be the only wound and was caused by the blow which had stunned him.

As Jovita chafed his hands and smoothed his forehead, he opened his eyes, and then looking about astonished at his surroundings, asked, "Where is the Christchild? Surely I have saved him."

The little one from the back of the horse began in his strange tones to sing the "Song of the Hemlock" in answer to Crescimir's enquiry.

"I hardly know where we are, for in the darkness and swift whirl of last night I lost my way," he said, sitting up. "I remember now that something struck me when the raft stopped. I thank God that the Christchild was not lost, dear little fellow."

"Christchild?" exclaimed Jovita, looking at him in surprise, "Have you given your boy that name?"

"I do not know, Señorita, who the child is, but he came to my door last night, Christmas Eve, and brought me some of the merriest hours I have had since I left old Illyria, and had not the flood carried away everything, I would have marked yesterday as one of the happiest in my life. He is a strange little fellow and will not, or else cannot speak, yet he sings beautifully in his own odd way as you hear him now. I called him Christchild as I knew no better name. Are you not the Señorita of El Tulucay? I know that horse which you have and have often seen him with a lady on his back flying over all the fields about here."

"Yes, I am Jovita of the Tulucay, and I know you now; you are called Crescimir the Illyrian, and I have been often to your cabin and sat beneath the great laurel while you were in the fields or at your work. I have often left flowers there at your door just for the pleasure of imagining the surprise when you should find them, and I always took the vegetables I found there, for I knew that they were for me. However, I never saw your face before this morning. You see I am little like our Californians, but my mother is from the States and believes in more freedom; she could not be better or kinder though she were a real Californian. If you are able we had better go up to the hacienda now, and after breakfast we will look about to see if assistance is needed along the river, for the flood was sudden and unlooked for."

Crescimir was not hurt and was able to walk slowly to the house. Jovita walked by his side, leading her horse, while the Christchild sat quietly in the saddle, nodding his head and winking like any sleepy child of this mortal world.

Both Crescimir and Jovita were silent during the walk, but their eyes often met, and Jovita would blush as she thought of her strange freak with the flowers and finding that the receiver was by no means the old man she had imagined him to be.

Crescimir was happy to think that he had not left his gifts unappreciated and only regretted that he had not put whole pumpkins there instead of onions.

"So you have no idea to whom the child belongs?" asked Jovita, as they neared the house. "He is strangely dressed and the frock is of an unfamiliar texture; he does not seem cold either, although he is so lightly clad. We must try to find his parents who, doubtless, are now anxiously searching for him or believing him drowned in last night's awful flood."

The strange little creature seemed now entirely to lose his sleepiness and broke into a merry laugh, sliding down from the saddle he capered madly around the two astonished spectators like a little elf blown about by the wind, his golden hair floating around him and the pink, little feet scarcely seeming to touch the grass.

"There has been a number of campers passing through the valley to settle north on the Caymus ranchos, this little sprite must be one of their children who has strayed away," said Jovita.

"Come little one, let us go into the house and have our breakfast."

The Christchild did not seem to understand her, for he continued his capering and wild antics.

"Stop, stop," exclaimed Crescimir in his native tongue, "stop and listen to what the beautiful Señorita says to thee. Come now into the house."

He ceased his play immediately and went before them up to the door, with tears in his eyes on account of Crescimir's rebuke. As they reached the veranda Crescimir caught the little elf up in his arms and kissed his rosy lips; the moment the child's feet touched the ground when Crescimir put him down, he put his hand over his mouth as if to keep the kiss warm and running to Jovita, she lifted him in her arms, as he signed her to do, when suddenly withdrawing his hand, he kissed her, looking back significantly and laughing.

Both Jovita and Crescimir knew what the child had intended to express and both blushed consciously, yet could but marvel at the acuteness of the little creature who so soon was able to read their hearts, even before they had perfectly known them themselves.

The mother of Jovita now came to the door and inviting them into the living room, the events of the past night were related and all that was known of the little waif.

Crescimir spent the day by the river searching for what might have been left on the banks by the flood. He learned that his raft had been carried out of the stream through a break in the bank, and much of the wreckage of his own house with it. Returning to the hacienda he discovered in a clump of bushes, over which the water had run when at its highest mark, the bodies of a man and woman entangled in the canvas cover of a camp wagon. It was evident to Crescimir from their dress that they were German emigrants.

With the help of some of the rancheros the bodies were carried to the house.

"They may be the parents of the little one," said Jovita's mother. "We will bring him here and see if he recognizes them; it seems cruel but it is the only way."

They brought the Christchild to the room where the bodies lay. When the little fellow saw them, he clung to Crescimir and uttering a moaning sound, yet seeming half like a laugh, he hid his eyes and would not look again.

"Are these thy parents little one?" asked Crescimir tenderly; the Christchild shook his head negatively and broke into hysterical sobs.

Though the Christchild had denied that these were the bodies of his parents, both Jovita, her mother and Crescimir felt certain that they were.

Crescimir remained that night at the Tulucay hacienda and early next morning the bodies were taken to the village and given burial in consecrated ground, as the cross which the woman wore and a medal of silver which the man carried showed them to be of the true church.

After the burial Crescimir returned to the rancheria. "I will be thy father now, little Christchild," said he as they stood at the well with Jovita, who had been filling the little olla for her mother's night drink.

The child looked up with a pleased smile and then turning to Jovita, asked with his bright eyes a question which words could not better have expressed.

Jovita replied softly as she looked down at the strange, wistful face, and felt the touch of Crescimir's hand on her own, "And I thy mother."

IV.

By the beginning of summer Crescimir's place had all been restored and the house rebuilt on the summit of the knoll, far away from any danger of another flood.

It was a pretty cottage now, in the new, American style with a trellis-porch over which passion vines spread in the profusion of first growth. The flower garden and the long lines and square beds of the vegetable garden looked fresh and bright down by the arroyo.

The house had been completed by the middle of January and Crescimir by careful and steady work had brought back his fields to their former state. The Christchild still lived with him, always as merry as the day was long. He was, as on the night of his arrival, still dressed in his little, white frock or shirt of strange texture, and he would wear nothing else, not even shoes.

Jovita's mother had, however, once made for him a suit, but when she tried to have him put it on, he objected so strenuously that the project had to be abandoned, for not even Crescimir's will, which usually was all that was needed on such occasions, had not in this case any power at all; so he ran quite wild about the gardens, the same pretty, little elf as ever.

He was extremely fond of the water and paddled in the arroyo all day long, so that even the little frock was for the greater time superfluous, and there was never any difficulty in having it for the old woman who came once a week from the village to do the washing. She often said that when she touched it, it gave her "goose flesh," the "feel" was so queer. She had never seen anything like it in all her long experience in her particular line of business.

Crescimir's visits to Tulucay were frequent now and the little Christchild always went with him, his greatest delight seeming to be to see Crescimir and Jovita together.

The day for the wedding was set to be the day before Christmas, for it seemed well that as that season had first made them known to each other, it should see them made man and wife.

The rainless summer and autumn passed and winter came with its green grass and new flowers.

Never had there been such a prosperous year for the Napa Valley, and the fields were fast blossoming with little white cottages, while golden vineyards were growing higher up the hillsides driving the chaparral back from its old inheritance as the Gringos did the natives. The town had increased to nearly twice its former size, so Crescimir's gardens were much sought, and he no longer was compelled to labour from sunrise till sunset to keep the weeds away, for now he was able to hire the hardest work done and enjoy the fruits of his first years' toil.

The month of December came and the leaves on the poplar trees in the village were turning golden, just lingering long enough to mingle lovingly for a while with the new-born green of winter, and then be hidden by the growth of broad leaved plants as soon as they had fallen brown upon the earth, producing that endless harmony of Californian nature, a life everlasting.

There were a few orange coloured poppies nodding in the mesas but violet star-flowers scattered over the lower meadows were powerful enough, by reason of their numbers, to conquer the colour of the grass, while the fields near the river were yellow with juicy cowslips.

Now the blue dome of St. Helena was not so often visible, for the clouds hovered about it filled with wealth giving rain.

Ploughing and planting had begun and in some places the grain had already started; blackbirds in hosts were perched on all the fences, watching the sowers and chattering saucily to each other as they snapped their bead-like eyes in anticipation of the feast so profusely spreading for them.

Over the low lands where the bay stretched its many arms in and out, offering to the ranchos its assistance to carry their abundant produce to a market, the marshes were red with short-growing sorrel, and the dark green of the tules along the edges fringed the silver indentations of the water in harmonious contrast.

All this did Jovita and Crescimir see from the veranda of Tulucay as with the Christchild by them they talked of the strange discovery and first sudden birth of their love, of how Jovita had first left the flowers at his door and how he had longed so much to know the one, the only one who had cheered his loneliness, and how he had loved the donor even before he had known that it was she.

Then they would talk of the terrible flood which had brought them together, and how each knew the other's love the moment their eyes had met, and of the mysterious little child who had been the medium of their first lovers' kiss.

They had become quite accustomed to the little elf's strange ways, and he no longer seemed to them to be the half supernatural creature he had at first appeared. Jovita's mother had at last discovered, she was sure, that the mysterious frock was nothing more nor less remarkable than a kind of goat hair woven carefully and fine.

So thus was the little elfin Christchild resolved by the power of familiarity into the orphan of some German emigrants who had lost their lives in the great flood; nevertheless, strangers never passed him without giving a second glance and never heard him sing in his sweet, odd tones, without wondering.

Crescimir and Jovita were married at Tulucay on the day before Christmas and walked over the fields to the new house on the knoll by the laurel tree, the Christchild going with them.

He had decorated his head and frock with blossoms of early mariposas (calochortus) in honour of the occasion, and his joy seemed uncontrollable and he skipped over the meadow scarcely seeming to tread upon the ground.

There was a bright fire in the cottage when they reached it; the fire was in an open fireplace similar to that which had been in the old cabin.

As they entered, the Christchild, running up to the hearth, pointed to the chimney piece, and then turning to Crescimir with a look which could not be misunderstood, began in his odd notes to sing.

Crescimir then first noticed that there was no hemlock branch above the hearth, so taking one from the other side of the room where they hung in festoons, he fastened it with a bunch of toyone berries over the chimney piece.

The sun was set and in the crimson glow with which the heavens were painted, just above the low, black hills, shone bright and silvery the Evening Star.

Crescimir, with Jovita leaning on his shoulder, stood at the west window looking out over the misty valley where the real seemed ghostlike in the gray evening haze, and even those things with which they were familiar, seemed in the fading light to take to themselves unknown forms.

"Strange world!" said Jovita, meditatively, "Real and Unreal so often blended that we can never say which is tangible and which is air."

"Look Jovita, look!" and Crescimir seizing her hand pointed out toward the garden.

They stood there gazing from the window, as if spellbound, until the crimson light faded from the sky and the clear star descended below the hills.

A bit of mist or fog, or what you will hovered about the garden and then gradually rising it became dissolved and was gone.

"Gone!" whispered Jovita, as the darkness shut out the valley from view. "Good little Christchild; but his memory shall ever be with us," answered Crescimir, as they sat side by side before the open fireplace.

———————

Everybody wondered where the little Christchild had gone, and search was made, but, of course, unsuccessfully; yet Crescimir and Jovita said nothing.

Thus, in time, people forgot about the tiny elf and now there are few who have even heard of Crescimir's guest.

The pretty cottage may to-day be seen on the knoll near the wonderful, wide-spreading laurel tree and every Christmas Eve upon the chimney piece of its open hearted hearth may be seen a dark, glossy branch of hemlock with a bunch of toyone.

Before the fire sit Crescimir and Jovita singing the little Christmas carrol of the Illyrian children. Sometimes they think that they hear a sweet, soft voice joining in harmony with their own, but yet they are not sure but that it may perhaps be only the music of their own happy hearts, and smiling at Jovita, who holds the little Crescimir in her arms, Crescimir the Illyrian points to the branch above the hearth while the little one opens his eyes in wonderment.

"Was he not, Jovita mia, like the affection which is seen by all the world between lovers before marriage? And then the world wonders where it has gone when the priest has pronounced the two as one. But we married lovers will never tell, for we are content to know that our Christchild has sunken deep into our hearts where his song inaudible to others is heard by us forever and ever."

Benícia's Letters.

After my aunt Benícia's death I found in her little desk a bundle of letters, which threw light upon the romance of her life, and on the reason perhaps of her refusing many offers which were known to have been made her by honoured Californians of the last generation. The letters are curious and interesting to me, and were written to my uncle by his chum, and enclosed many sketches.

The letters are in Spanish, but for your better understanding I have translated them with all their strange expressions as best I can.

At first I thought that I would destroy them, but as most of my friends who read them now, have long known my aunt Benicia, I feel sure that they will be, even in these practical days, interested and touched by the revelation they so suggest of a life-long love which filled the heart of the good, little woman, who is at last at rest.

Grünen Markt.
Würzburg, 20th October, 18—.

Dear José:

How dull life here is, I cannot bear to look forward to the time so far ahead when I shall have done with the University, not that I shall be at all unhappy to leave and return to my dear California, but the twelve or sixteen months between now and then, make me shudder to think of.

My time is quite free now and I make many pleasure walks to Zell and the Hochberg, while almost every day finds me at some time on the Nicholaus Berg enjoying its ever lovely views of the green Maine valley, which however is now taking on its first autumnal tints.

Today I come from the stone quarry, which lies on the road to the Hochberg, where I have been chatting with the workmen and making a few sketches to send home to Benicia; the day has been one of the pleasantest I have known, just one of those mild autumn days we love so much in Santa Clara when her hills are clothed in their warmest colours and the big leaves are first falling from the fig trees. Ah, I did wish to be back again to walk with you along the dry Francisquito and gather the first golden poppies for Benicia's black hair. Yes, of course, I should be contented with these world-known beauties which I have about me, nevertheless, it is a pleasure to recall those happy days now that I am here alone on the continent of Europe. The warmth of our Californian sun must have entered our very hearts, for nowhere in all the world but there are found no strangers.

The grapes are not all picked as yet, and the vineyards are lively indeed with gaily dressed peasant girls, cutting and tying up the vines for the winter. There is a great difference between Catholic and Lutheran Germany in this one regard of dress; in all the Protestant districts the prevailing colour is a dull blue, while in Catholic parts the dress seems to have no end of colour and brilliant adornment; for an artist the latter is more pleasing, but for such a thoughtful moralist as yourself, I know the peasant girls in blue frocks would be preferable.

There are very few students in the city now and scarcely a traveller is to be seen, except now and then a stray one may be noticed wandering about the old cathedral or counting the restored statues on the river bridge. I always feel a longing to speak to these late birds of passage for they look so forlorn without their mates, that they make me think of my own sad plight so far away from you all; when the lectures begin I hope that I will be more satisfied than I am now.

Every day I go to Vespers at one of the churches, and I enjoy this bit of the day more than you could believe. It is beautiful just at dusk to enter the church in the Market Place, which is near my hotel, and there in the gloom, lighted only by the tapers at the shrines and where some of the worshipers are kneeling, each with a small wax light to illumine the Prayer Books, to bow with them and receive the blessing from the priest and to be touched by the Holy Water; then the Ave Maria, how I love to hear it chanted with such heartfelt praise by the old and trembling men and women, who throw their whole spirit into the melody. The melody, I know, could not bear cold criticism, but when I kneel there beneath the great, gray vault and see their breath ascending in the cold air, bearing like incense their prayers to Heaven, and hear the subdued strains of the organ, I feel that it is not the music of this world, and my heart is moved and I join in the grand hymn, mingling my soft Latin words with their glorious German.

The priest has passed down the aisle and sprinkled the Holy Water over us with the aspergil, the boys bearing the censers, preceding him have passed from sight with him behind the dark curtain at the Chancel door; there is a shuffling noise of the departing worshipers and I am alone.

Far away, before the golden Altar hangs a taper which throws a red glow into all the darkness, it is the Sacred Heart of Jesus, ever burning amid the gloom of sin. As my eyes become accustomed to the dim light, I can discern a female figure robed in gray, standing before the shrine of the Virgin, I cannot see the face though I often try, but whenever she becomes aware of my presence, she leaves the cathedral by the little door to the right which opens into the small court. This occurs every night, and though I have often tried to meet her by going out by the other door and around the front, I have as yet, not succeeded.

But enough of that now; today as I returned from my walk, I saw as I was crossing the bridge one of the first Californian women I have seen for a long time; I know that she was Californian or Mexican for there was more life in the eye than we see in the quiet, expressionless beauties of the rest of the world. I do not know why I must ever have this face in my mind since I met the fair one on the bridge; she looked at me directly in the eyes, and I feel sure that I have met her sometime before. I know the face; there is a strange drooping about the eyelids, which to me adds a charm to the whole appearance. I do wish I could think where in the world I have seen her. I am going to search the hotel books to-morrow for I will not rest until I find out her name. It was almost dark, however, when we met, and she was going toward the opposite side of the Maine where there are no foreign hotels.

I surmise, and suppose, and guess, but all to no purpose, while that one look seems to be planted indelibly upon my mind. I would give anything to see her again; I can think of nothing now, for the strange, inexpressible fascination of those eyelids has me entirely captive. Where have we met? Try and think, my dear boy, of some one of our acquaintance who tallies with my description; about my height, black hair, a white, unusually white face, finely marked eyebrows and the drooping lids, which when raised, disclose large, brilliant, yet languid, blue eyes,—I cannot give the picture to suit me, but you note the strange paleness and the eyes, and you must remember if you have ever met her.

I often go to the little opera house, where the music is of the best, yet I cannot enjoy myself, for, as ever I am alone; all I can do is just to think and think and imagine things to interest me through the dreary time. What strange fantasies I have brought up in my life! You know some of them, and it is quite true as you wrote in your last that translation from Hawthorne, "His caprices had their origin in a mind that lacked the support of an engrossing purpose and feelings that preyed upon themselves for lack of other food."

I try to interest myself in the things about me, but I am a dreamer. I wonder often what my life will come to in the end, of what use I shall be. No, it is not good that I should be alone; now, however, since I have seen the unknown beauty, I will not have to search my mind for subjects to keep it occupied, for Señorita California is quite a solid damsel and far from ethereal, and not at all ghostly, only that look about the eyes when the lids are drooping, and the complexion.

Don't forget my usual token to Benicia and give her the sketches, but of course no word of the girl; women never understand such things properly.

B. L. M.

Joaquin.

On the Nicholaus Berg.

22nd October, 18—.

Dear José:

This morning early, I took my walk as usual to the Chapel on the hill; the day was as fine as the last three have been and I began to feel better contented with so much Californian weather to help me.

Yesterday I did not think so much of the bridge beauty but today her strange features have come to me with double vividness, and it was to escape from this that I took the walk so very early this morning. I brought my sketch-book with me and expected to pass the whole day on the hill and in the woods just beyond.

The little, old woman who sweeps away the dry leaves from the steps so ruthlessly, smiled more than usual when I gave her the customary two pfennigs. I can never understand how the poor creature wages such a heartless war against these dying leaves of Autumn; it seems that she should have a sisterly feeling for them, knowing that she is herself so near to her own December.

The Stations of the Cross are arranged in little shrines on the many terraces which adorn the castle side of the hill; it is a pretty thought, bordering the path to the chapel with these stone pictures, most of them representing Christ's long, weary journey up Mount Calvary. There are always to be found before these shrines, people, mostly the peasantry, praying aloud, and here and there many a time I have seen them ascending the toilsome road on their knees.

What a grand view one has from the summit; the wide valley of the Maine not yet brown, but smiling as it always does in its green beauty, far into December. The lumber rafts are floating lazily down, as it were in a dream, little thinking that in a few more hours they will have reached their journey's end, there to be broken. They are like myself somewhat, who am just as lazily, uselessly and alone wandering through life to the ending sooner or later; it is hard to go against the stream and the river is long and lovely, so I will float on just a little farther.

I made a sketch of Würzburg with its many spires and domes, which I enclose for Benicia, and then turned my attention to the Chapel with which I am always delighted; the frescoes in the dome are good and I never tire of sitting and looking up at them while I listen to the dull chanting of the Capuzin monks behind the iron grating to the right.

I have often had conversation with these monks whom I meet walking in the garden, and find them pleasant and entertaining, and far from being the gloomy mortals some people think them to be.

Nicholaus Berg.

Night.

Dear José:

Before I had finished my letter, Brother Andreas, with whom I am better acquainted than with the others, came to me and asked me to walk with him; he is not a German, but is from Spain, so you see I find use for my mother tongue where I little expected to need it. Brother Andreas speaks German of course, as he has been here some twenty years, and tells me he is quite contented with his life, never having a desire for sunny Spain, saying that all the home he has is beyond this world; I wish that I might feel as contented as the old Capuzin.

But you are curious to know why I am here at this time, and I will hasten to tell you what the strange cause is.

We walked about the Chapel and through parts of the garden where I had never been before, Brother Andreas relating to me the history of the city and the little Chapel. By this time we had wandered to the front of the building, and Brother Andreas raising his arm pointed to the face of the church over the door and repeated, "Refugium Peccatorum, Consolatrix Afflictorum, Sancta Maria, Ora Pro Nobis."

I did not look up at first, my attention at the time being directed to a company of peasants in the neighbouring vineyard, but at the words "Sancta Maria," I raised my eyes to the face of the church, and, oh my God, what did I see!

"Ora pro nobis," broke unintentionally from my lips, I clung convulsively to the arm of the good, old priest, my eyes were riveted upon the niche above the door, for there looking down on me, her eyes strangely drooping, her hands folded across her breast, stood the woman whom day before yesterday I met on the bridge; I say stood the woman, but it was only a statue carved in gray stone, an image of the Virgin, such as we see every day in the churches; this, however, was somewhat different, as it held no infant Christ in its arms, and then the face, that was not the face which should be given to Mary, the Mother of our Saviour.

No, the more I see those eyes, which I at first so much admired, the more I hate their look, but also strange to say, the more I am fascinated.

In a few moments I had recovered my usual composure enough to assure Brother Andreas that the cause of my strange behaviour was a sudden illness to which I was often subject, when tired, but the good man shook his head sadly and said, "No, my child, you have seen something supernatural, which has disturbed you; it is well that I am here." With that, he immediately made the Sign of the Cross and drew me into the chapel where he made some use of the Holy Water which I did not understand, nor did I care, for the sudden fright which had stopped my heart in its beating, now that all was over, sent the blood rushing through my veins with frightful rapidity making my head ache so terribly that I thought that I must die.

It was dark, the next I knew, the room was strange to me; A Crucifix hung on the wall, before which a single, dim oil lamp was burning, before this was a monk at prayer;—it seemed like a dream to me, it could not be real.

After awhile I moved, and the monk rose and came to me, showing, in the flickering light, the fatherly features of Brother Andreas.

"My child," he said, taking my hand in his, "I am happy that you are of our flock, for I can help you; I know your thoughts; it is well to think now when all is still. I will not urge you, but Christ is ever seeking for your soul; come to the true light of the Church where he may find you."

I made confession and received absolution, and he, making the Sign of the Cross, went from the room.

Presently I heard the monotonous chant of the monks in the Chapel and knew it was midnight. I have written this to you hurriedly on paper I have in my portfolio. The chanting is over and Brother Andreas' step is audible in the echoing corridor. Good Night.

Besa la mano,

Joaquin.

_____

Nicholaus Berg.

30th October, 18—.

Dear José:

I am still at the cloister, though I have done nothing it seems to me during the past week but sleep, and am hardly strong enough now to carry the pen over the paper as I write to you.

The statue over the door stands there as it ever has, but it is too far away for me to see the awful eyes, so I can say nothing about them. But now my dear friend I have something more wonderful than ever to tell you.

Every night when the moon shines, this image of the Virgin comes down from her niche and wanders about the church; I have seen her four or five times, and she has often come under my window in these lone walks, and once I spoke to her, but the moment my voice sounded on the night air she was gone, and the same gray, stone image stood silent and dead in the niche.

What can I think of all this? I could not believe if any one should tell me of these things, but what I see with my own eyes I certainly cannot doubt.

The Brother Andreas is very good to me, and my box has been brought from the hotel to the cloister, so my room is as cheerful as possible with all your pictures around me.

How I wish that you were here, or I could hear from you, but never, my dear boy will that time come, I fear; I have given up the idea of ever having so great a pleasure in this world. I cannot write more now as I am too weak. Good night and greet Benicia for me.

———

31st October.

It is very late, but I must write now or never. To-night the image was stranger than ever, and for the first time I heard its voice, and oh, it sounded too sweetly to me as I sat by the window and looked out over the city as the moon rose above the hills to the east.

The Brothers were chanting at the time, and their deep base came in ever and ever so beautifully between the stanzas which the Virgin sung, and as she sung, she came down from her station slowly, as if there were steps in the air and she could tread upon them. The words were as weird as the scene.

"The silver moon is slowly, slowly rising

The night is clear and all the clouds are fled,

Their midnight prayer the weary monks are chanting;

Now I may leave my cold and stony bed."

Then the monks chanted in their low, measured tones,

"Sancta Maria, ora pro nobis!

Mater Christi, ora, ora!"

"Cursed be my lot, but useless is repining,

Here must I stay till dreary day is gone,

Living only in the pale moon's shining;

To-night my hated penance though is done.

Gaily, gaily, gaily I'll live

Though I be but a spirit of air;

Every pleasure the world can give

Shall be mine while the moon shines fair.

The Devil in Hell has promised me

That if I gain him a soul

I shall be forever from that time free,

So long as the Rhine shall run to the sea

And the Maine shall Rhineward roll."

And from the heights above the echo came,—"Roll—roll."

Then running lightly to the wall, which is on the river side, she leaned over and sung in a high, unearthly, wild voice, while her dark hair waved in the night wind,

"Beautiful river rushing on,

Touched with light by the silver moon,

Grant me now this simple boon.

Let thy merry spirits come,

And elfin dancers with beating drum,

Here with me for the wild night long,

To dance and whirl with eldrich song

Till the moon shall faint and her light be gone."

Then running merrily to the other side nearer my window, she sung in the same wild key, as she turned her face to the forest,

"Spirits of the black larch-wood

Come to-night to dance and sing,

Come and all thy flowers bring,

Come and gaily join our ring,

Come upon thy fleetest wing,

Come, oh come, ere the moon be fading."

The low chanting of the Monks ceased, and as I opened my window wider I could hear, like the higher notes of an organ, voices rising from the river and mingling in heavenly harmony; I could not at first catch the words, but the sweet, divinely sweet strains came nearer and nearer, and then with the same inexpressible gentleness, softly as if wafted from the angelic chorus came the rich, low notes from the forest, like the humming of bees, the sighing of hemlocks, or that sweet, strange sound we ever hear in the ocean shell. The voices came nearer and I could hear the wild, free words long before the singers were in the court.

"We are coming from the forest,

All laden with flowers,

With bright, crimson flowers

All sparkling with dew."

Then from the river rose the song:

"We come from the water

With bright, polished pebbles,

With white, glittering pebbles,

Our love-gift to you."

The singing now was in the very garden, but I could not see the singers, though I knew that they were there, for the strange creature-image whirled about the court, laughing and nodding on every side, while the music grew each moment louder and wilder, when suddenly all was still, and the image pausing in the middle of the court began with many odd gestures this weird song:

"What am I? Who am I? Where did I come from?

What, who and where—well, no human knows;

Ye though my loved ones know what to answer,

My pale face ye follow wherever it goes.

My home's in the forest, my home's in the city,

Wherever the terror of loneliness lies,

And woe be to him who when out in the moonlight

Catches the glance of my soul-piercing eyes.

By day I am stone

By night I have breath,

And those whom I meet, know the sister of Death."

"Curse you!" I shrieked, leaning from the window, and all was gone; the statue was in its niche again, the Maria Virgo Sancta. I staggered back from the window and was received almost breathless from excitement in the arms of Brother Andreas who entered the room just then.

"My child, you should not sit by an open window; I fear that you have done yourself an injury already." He laid me down on the bed and when I awoke he was gone, and now I am writing off this scrap of a letter for you my dear friend. How I long to see you, and oh, why can I not have you here! Would to God that I had not met the woman on the bridge. My friend, my José, I dare not tell you what I fear; those eyes were upon me, those fatal eyes. No, no I will not keep it from you, I will tell you all and leave you the terrible duty of telling Benicia.

My dear boy, I am growing colder each moment; my hand trembles as I write this, my last letter; I pray that I may have strength to finish it. The river was not so long as I expected, and now my poor raft is breaking. Nor would I live, for now I know who has power over me, I know now whose were those drooping eyelids; it is better not to live, for I have not strength to conquer them.

It is autumn, the last leaves are falling, the cold winter is coming, but I shall not be here to dread its cold. My winter is on me now, and may God grant that through it I come to the eternal spring. All that I want is to see Benicia and you once more, but that cannot be. Now a last, long farewell to Benicia; I can write no more, I am too cold. The raft is broken; the journey was not long.

God bless you, good bye; I am going to lie down now. Give the ruby ring, which I wear, to dear Benicia as a memory of me; and tell Beni—

———————

Here was the ending of the letter in the unfinished name of his loved one.

The End